TIDES
EXPLORER
Guide

WILLIAM THOMSON

Imray

William Thomson FRGS is an author, artist and adventurer.

He is founder of *Tide School* and a Fellow of the Royal Geographical Society. William is author and illustrator of *The Book of Tides* and *The World of Tides*, and regularly writes for magazines including Yachting Monthly, Coast, Outdoor Swimmer and Sailing Today.

William lives full-time aboard his yellow catamaran *Luna* with his partner Naomi, their children Ottilie and Arva, and the family's rescued Mallard duck 'Herby'. The crew are currently on a long-term circumnavigation, taking time to fully explore the places they visit while William writes and runs his *Tide School,* teaching people how to 'Seas The Power'.

In addition to sailing, William is a trained PADI Rescue Diver, sea swimmer and surfer. This multi-dimensional approach to adventures brings a practical experience to William's work, which is shared through this series of Explorer Guides - made for anyone who enjoys the sea.

Published by
Imray, Laurie, Norie and Wilson Ltd
Wych House
The Broadway
St Ives
Cambridgeshire
PE27 5BT

+44 (0) 1480 462114
ilnw@imray.com
2021

© William Thomson, 2021

All rights reserved. No part of this publication may be reproduced, transmitted or used in any form by any means, electronic or mechanical, including photocopy, recording or anyinformation storage and retrieval systems, without permission in writing from the Publisher.

British Library Cataloguing in Publication Data.
A catalogue record for this title is available from the British Library.

ISBN 978 178679 292 1

Printed and bound in Croatia by Denona

6	INTRODUCTION	
12	CHANGES WITH **TIME**	
28	CHANGES WITH **PLACE**	
38	**CLUES** FOR EXPLORERS	
52	**PHENOMENA** MADE BY TIDES	
58	TIDE DICTIONARY	

We live in a fascinating age of information where accurate forecasts streamed to our phones can tell us exactly what the winds, waves, tides and streams will be doing every hour of the coming days. But what these forecasts do not tell us is how these conditions interact with each other and the coast to create a specific sea state at a certain time and place. The purpose of this series is to fill that gap, equipping you with the skill to take a forecast and use that knowledge to predict what to expect where and when.

Why is this important? Because if you know what is going to happen in an hour around the headland, or tomorrow in the bay, you will be better informed to make decisions that enhance your safety and performance. Those hidden dangers lurking beneath the surface will be less of a threat because you were aware of them long in advance, while precious windows of opportunity will always be made best use of. In short, with these guides at your side you will be one step closer to being in the right place at the right time, safely bypassing the wrong places at the wrong times.

To the untrained eye, the sea can seem like a chaotic environment, puzzling and unpredictable. But with guidance, a natural order appears from the chaos. There is always an explanation for why something is happening, and it is usually a blend of simple factors coinciding - the shape of coastline, time of day, weather conditions, moon phase. In this collection of books we will explore all these factors one at a time, analysing their individual effect on the sea's moods. To achieve this, each guide focuses on a different element (Tides, Streams, The Moon, Winds, Waves, Rips, Clouds, Currents, Stars) and they are organised into two main sections; 'Changes with Time' and 'Changes with Place', with each page analysing the effects of a single variable.

Infographics are an integral role in this work because they are so effective at helping to explain concepts. But when it comes to cycles, such as the moon orbiting the earth or tide waves spinning around oceans, a stationary image can only show one moment in the cycle and you need to visualise the rest. This can be difficult, so to make learning easier there is a collection of DIY models to accompany these guides. The idea is for you to download the designs for free at www.tidalcompass.com using the code EXPLORERGUIDES and assemble the models at home, using them alongside these pages to better understand natural processes.

▶

If you are reading this book you are aware of the sea's power. Although we can train our bodies to be as strong as possible, in a strength contest with the ocean we will lose every time. Even the strongest boats may be overwhelmed by a rogue wave. But luckily we have a secret weapon - the power of our minds. Instead of trying to achieve our objectives with brawn, we can use our brains. These guides will help you to do this by deepening your understanding of nature's forces and sharing ways to harness this energy to your advantage, going further and faster while consuming less of your own precious energy. If our ultimate goal is to be summed up in three words, it must surely be 'Seas The Power'.

William Thomson
Aboard *Luna*, at sea

At school we are taught that the moon's gravity makes two bulges in our oceans and the earth spins within this watery embryo to give us high and low tide.

The theory goes that every six hours the earth makes a quarter turn on its axis, moving you between A (low tide) and B (high tide) on the illustration. While this helps explain why there are two highs and two lows every day, the explanation has one major flaw; it relies on there being no land on earth. In reality the conglomeration of continents and islands scattered around the world's seas means this theory is not an accurate description of what really happens, so is of little practical use to you.

In this book you are going to learn what really makes the tide and discover practical knowledge you can apply to your adventures. While the information in the following pages has been around for hundreds, even thousands, of years, it has been scattered through complicated books, marine manuals, academic studies and nautical charts. The idea of the *Tides Explorer Guide* is to fit the jigsaw pieces together, creating order out of chaos and giving you a simple-to-use guide guaranteed to boost your sea-safety and performance.

CHANGES WITH TIME

If you stay in one place for a long time you will notice hourly, weekly and monthly changes in the tide. While these follow a natural cycle that can be predicted years in advance, the weather on a particular day can have a huge effect on what happens to the tide.

In this section we will investigate the astronomical and meteorological conditions that make the tide change with time, exploring tips to help you predict what will happen next.

6 o'clock

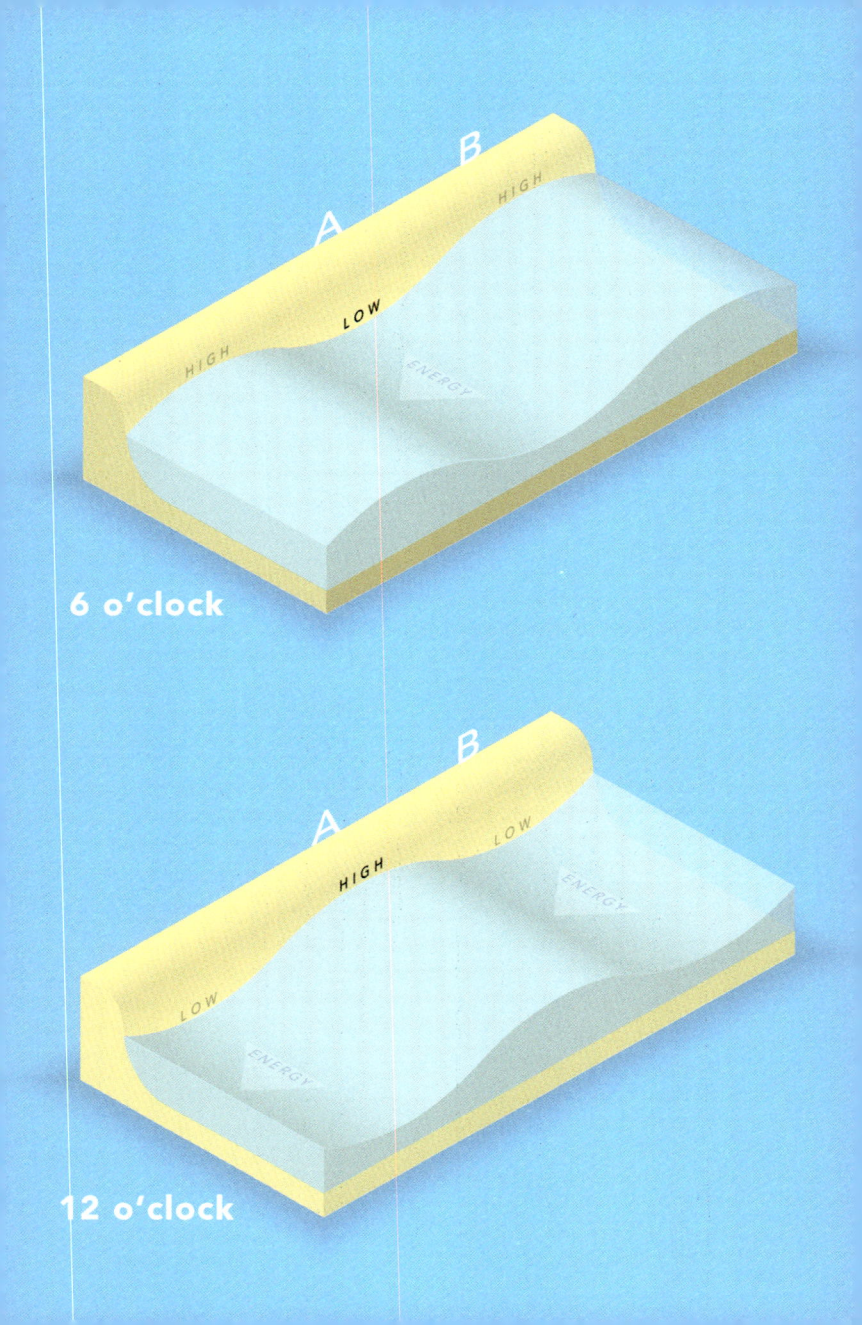

A B
HIGH
LOW
HIGH
ENERGY

12 o'clock

A B
LOW
HIGH LOW
ENERGY
ENERGY

High Tide is the peak of a very long wave

Tides are made by waves flowing around the world's oceans; the distances between peaks and troughs are too vast for us to see with the naked eye (they range from hundreds to thousands of kilometres), but when a trough passes you experience low tide and just over six hours later a peak brings high tide. The reason these waves return every day is because they travel in great circles around ocean and sea basins (anti-clockwise in the northern hemisphere and clockwise in the southern hemisphere). To work out the direction of your local tide wave, look at the tide times for the places either side of you; the one that gets high tide first is the direction the wave will be coming from.

The depth of water determines how fast a tide wave travels. In the deepest ocean around the abyssal plain, the peaks of tide waves can move at speeds over 1,000km/h - but when they reach the shallow continental shelf they slow down to around 100km/h. To calculate the speed that a tide wave travels along your coast, simply compare the tide times between two places and divide the distance by time difference. For example, if high tide at Place B is at 6 o'clock and high tide at Place A is at 12 o'clock, and they are 600km apart, the wave must travel around 100km/h.

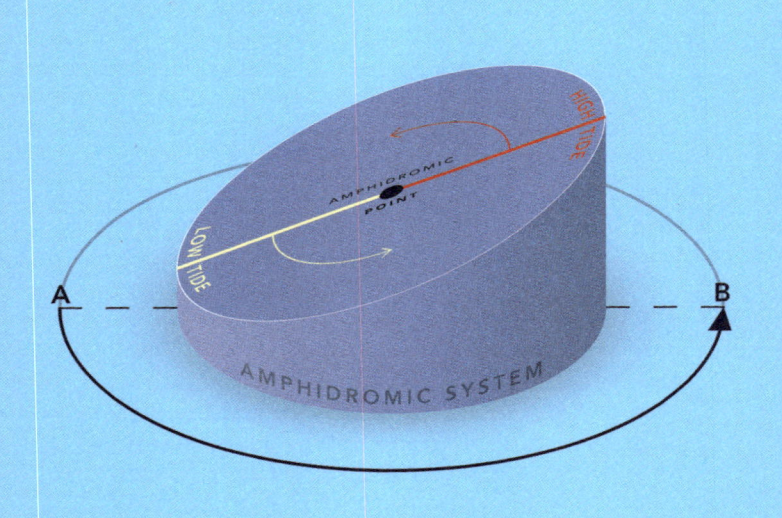

IN 6 HOURS LOW TIDE WILL BE AT B
HIGH TIDE WILL BE AT POSITION A

Tide waves are made by 'Amphidromic Systems'

Tide Waves are made by Amphidromic Systems, named from the Latin words *amphi* (around) and *dromic* (running). In essence, these are bodies of energy shaped by the gravitational pull from the moon and set in motion by the spinning of earth on its axis. A simple way to imagine one is to think of a disc titled at an angle and spinning around a central point once every 12 hours 25 minutes (the time between high tides). The beauty of Amphidromic Systems is that they are in sync across all the world's oceans, with high points meeting seamlessly to create the peaks of tide waves.

In the North Atlantic, there is a single amphidrome travelling anti-clockwise. From Land's End, the peak travels up to Iceland and Greenland then down the coast of Canada and the eastern seaboard of the US, before travelling across to North Africa and up the coast of Europe, returning to Lands End every 12 hours 25 minutes. To better visualise how these Amphidromic Systems make the tide rise and fall, you can download the kit for this model for free at www.tidalcompass.com and make it yourself, spinning the disc to simulate how high tide travels around the Atlantic ocean.

50 MINS

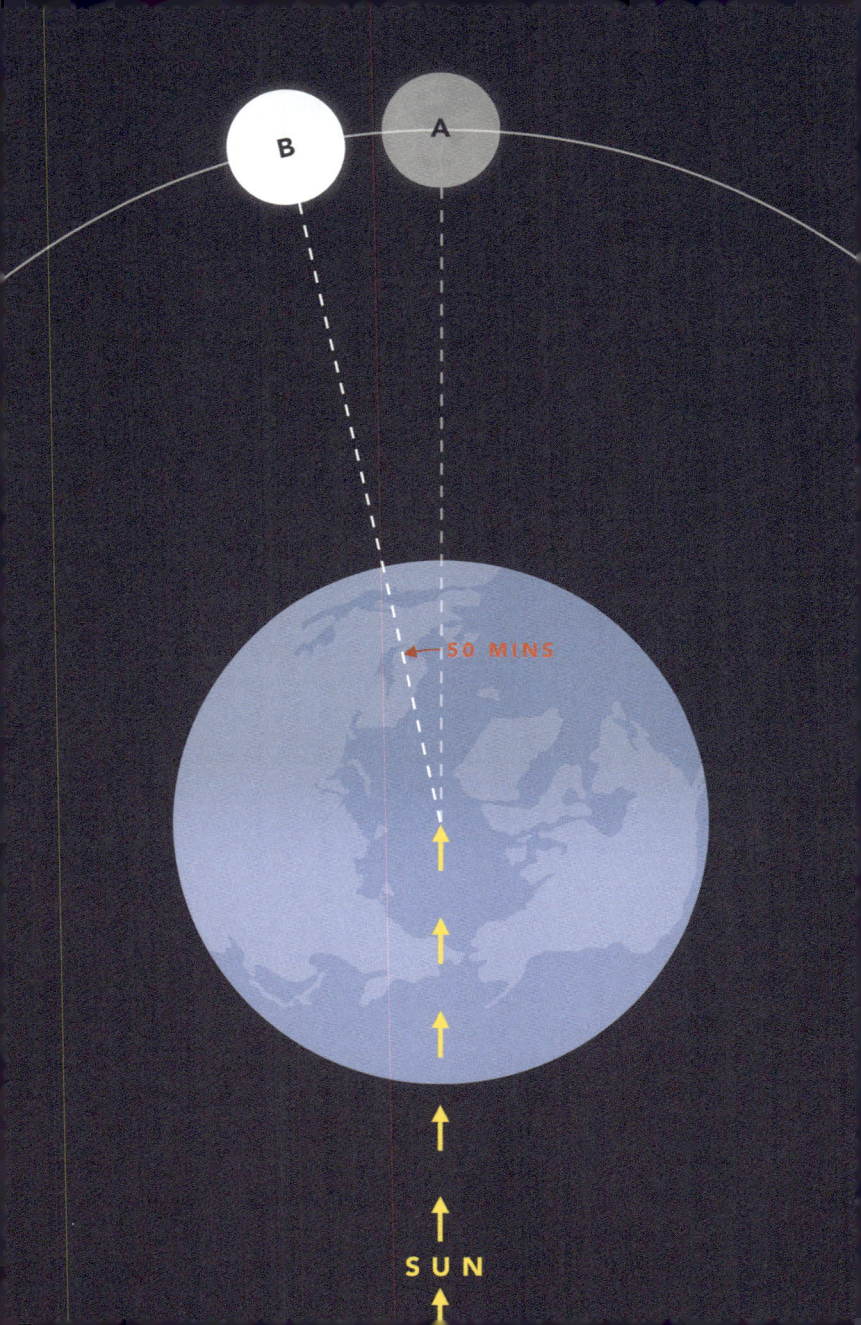

SUN

High Tide happens 50 minutes later every day

A 'day' is measured as the time it takes your meridian (an imaginary line on earth running from north to south pole and passing through your position) to line up with the sun or moon as the earth rotates on its axis. While a solar day takes 24 hours, a lunar day (the time for a full tidal cycle of two highs and two lows) is 50 minutes longer. This is because in the 24 hours it takes the earth to make a full 360-degree spin on its axis, the moon has moved around 12 degrees on its orbit (from A to B), so it takes another 50 minutes for your meridian to realign with the moon and start a new tidal day.

A quirk of this daily delay is that high tide happens 6 hours later every week (50 mins. x 7 days = 350 mins. = approx. 6 hours). Because 6 hours is the time between high and low tides, and the main moon phases are a week apart, it means the tide times are mirrored every week. So if it is high tide at 12 o'clock on the Full Moon, it will be low tide at 12 o'clock on the weeks either side (when half the moon is visible), and it will be back to 12 o'clock on the New Moon. To master this technique fully you need some knowledge of the moon, which can be achieved with help from *The Moon Explorer Guide*.

■ = **MAX.** TIDE INTENSITY
■ = **MIN.** TIDE INTENSITY

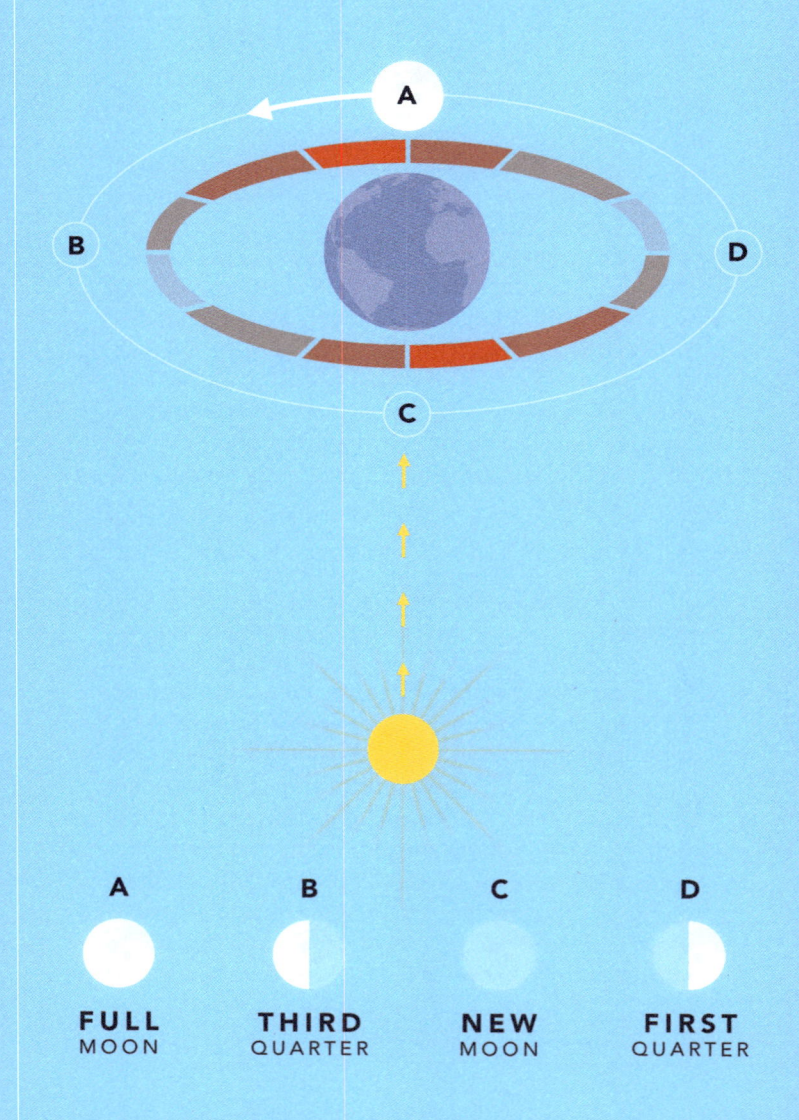

A	B	C	D
FULL MOON	**THIRD** QUARTER	**NEW** MOON	**FIRST** QUARTER

Tides are stronger just after the Full Moon and New Moon

Because the sun exerts less than half the gravitational force as the moon it has little effect on daily tides - but it does play an important role in the monthly tidal cycle. At the Full Moon (A) and New Moon (C), when the sun and moon are in line with earth, their forces are combined and tides are stronger, a period called springs. There are two common misconceptions with spring tides; firstly, the name misleads many to believe they only happen in spring. Secondly, a time lag with the sea means that tides are actually strongest 36 hours after alignment and not on the actual days of New Moon and Full Moon.

At springs, amphidromes become more 'tilted' and this results in steeper tide waves with higher peaks and deeper troughs. With more water flowing between high and low tide every six hours, everything becomes more intense and dangers are heightened. If this intensity makes a place too hazardous to explore, one option is to wait a week for when the moon is perpendicular to the sun and earth. This is when their combined forces are reduced and tides are weaker, a time called neaps when everything is mellower and risks are reduced.

B

A —SYZYGY—

A = **PERIGEE** (356,500KM)

B = **APOGEE** (406,700KM)

Tides are strongest 3-6 times a year when there is a 'supermoon'

The moon's orbit is not perfectly circular; instead, it is elliptical. This means there is a day each month when it is furthest away and a day when it is closest to earth. The moment it is closest is called perigee, and because of the way the earth moves around the sun, there are 3-6 days every year when perigee happens at exactly the same time as the moon being in line with the sun and earth (the wonderfully named syzygy). The effect is a 'supermoon' and perigean spring tides, which are supercharged springs caused by the heightened gravitational pull from the moon because of its proximity to the earth.

If you look at a chart or tide forecast you will see the abbreviations MLWN, MLWS and LAT. These refer to the average heights of low water (low tide) at a particular moon phase. MLWN is 'Mean Low Water Neaps', MLWS is 'Mean Low Water Springs', and LAT is 'Lowest Astronomical Tide'. LAT is what we get close to when there is a perigean spring just after the supermoon. While an astronomical almanac will give you plenty of warning for the phenomena, nature's clue is the moon being 15% bigger and 30% brighter – so if you see a big and bright moon, expect big and boisterous tides.

HIGHER PRESSURE = LOWER TIDES

TYPICAL WEATHER

SUNNY SKIES — LOW WINDS*

*Winds are stronger when isobars on synoptic chart are closer together

VERTICAL MOVEMENT OF AIR
COLD(ER) AIR SINKING

— ASTRONOMICALLY PREDICTED TIDE —
TIDE PUSHED DOWN BY AIR PRESSURE

WIND DIRECTION ON A SYNOPTIC CHART

H

In the Northern Hemisphere, winds blow clockwise around a high pressure system and anti-clockwise around a low

Tides are higher on days with lower air pressure

Meteorological factors have a huge effect on the tide, particularly on days when extreme high or low pressure systems pass through. When there is high pressure (made by cold air sinking) this literally pushes down the surface of the sea, giving us lower tides. In contrast, when there is low pressure (made by warm air rising) this allows the sea to rise up, resulting in higher tides. Average air pressure at sea is 1013mb and as a basic rule of thumb the tide will rise by 1cm for every 1millibar drop in atmospheric pressure.

With this knowledge you can quickly gauge the tide simply by observing the weather. If there are clear blue skies it is likely to be high pressure, so you would expect lower tides. But if it is cloudy and rainy, the probability is that there is low air pressure, so tides will be higher. The consequence of these meteorological factors is that you must take the tide prediction with a pinch of salt, because the actual tide height is rarely exactly what is written on your tide table or app. To better understand the relationship between tides and pressure, you can download, print and assemble the model in this diagram, pushing and pulling the tab to see the connection between the two.

ONSHORE **OFF**SHORE

Tides are higher on days with onshore winds

When the wind is blowing onto the shore it pushes water up the beach, making higher tides. But when the wind is blowing offshore, it pushes the sea away to keep the tide at bay. Usually the wind direction is an effect of large-scale weather systems with a consistent wind direction all day, however at certain times of year (summertime in mid-latitudes) a sea-breeze often develops through the day. This results in onshore winds being strongest in the mid-afternoon, so you would expect the tides around this time of day to be higher than predicted. But at night the breeze turns offshore, growing in strength around the early hours leading up to dawn, so tides would be lower than forecasted around sunrise.

A side-effect of onshore winds is that they make high tide arrive earlier. If an adventure is dependant on timing the tides precisely and leaving a specific time before high tide, you can set off earlier and be confident that there will be enough water under your keel. On the other hand, if there is an offshore wind then tides are delayed, so there is no point rushing to get afloat because you may need to wait a little longer for high water.

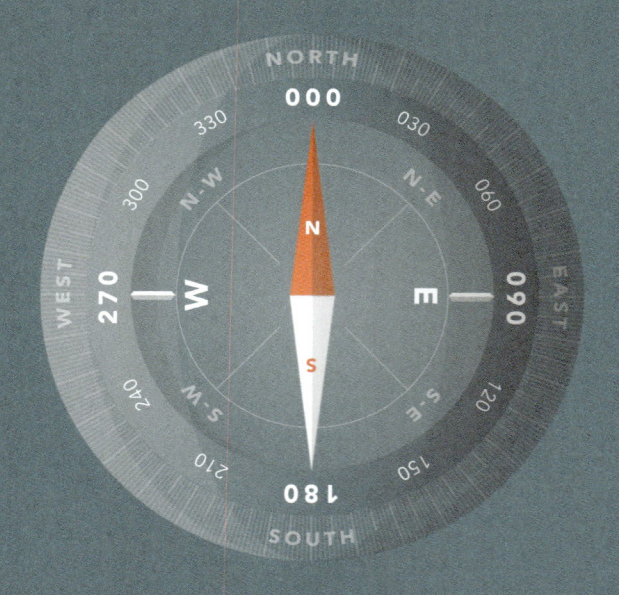

CHANGES WITH

PLACE

The shape of coastline and depth of water have a huge impact on the intensity of tides. In some places the tide height can double as you go around the corner, while worldwide ranges vary from just a few centimetres to over 15 metres.

In this section we will explore what makes these changes, helping you anticipate what to expect from one place to the next.

FLAT BEACH

STEEP CLIFFS

LOW TIDE | **HIGH** TIDE

TIDE GOES <u>IN</u>

TIDE GOES <u>UP</u>

On a shallow gradient seabed, the tide is more dramatic than on a steeply sloping seabed

In fact, the two shorelines may have exactly the same tidal range, but on a shallow beach a small drop in the tide will expose a larger area of beach. In contrast, the same fall in the sea level on a nearby steep beach might have little noticeable effect. For example, if the gradient is 1:1, a 1-metre drop in the tide will only expose 1 metre of the beach. But in a shallow bay with a 1:100 slope, the same fall of tide will make the waterline recede by 100 metres, and a 10-metre tide will go back 1 kilometre.

The skill is being able to predict the seabed angle at high tide; this helps you judge what the environment will look like in 6 hours time and whether the change will affect you. Clues of a steep beach include cliffs with intense waves suddenly jacking up and breaking at their base, with dark blue water close to shore. In contrast, on a shallow beach you are more likely to see piers or jetties extending out to sea, shallow-faced mellow waves gently peeling a long way from the beach, and sandy coloured water. In these places you would expect a dramatic transition between high and low tide, making the place almost unrecognisable.

SMALLER TIDES

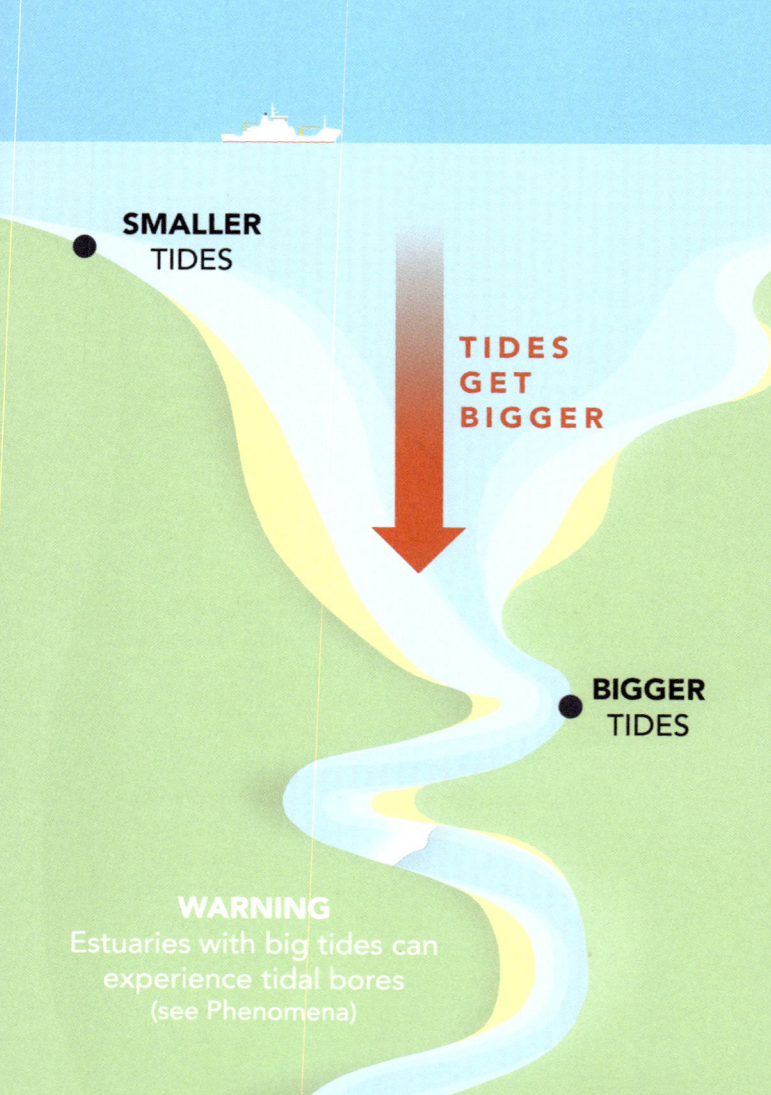

TIDES GET BIGGER

BIGGER TIDES

WARNING
Estuaries with big tides can experience tidal bores
(see Phenomena)

Funnel-shaped bays and estuaries often have the biggest tides

This is due to a funnelling effect where the coastline steadily narrows and the seabed gradually shallows, concentrating water into the narrowest part at the end of the 'funnel'. The shape of some bays – in particular their length/width ratio – can create a bathtub-like phenomenon called resonance, where the timing of tide waves surging in and out of the bay coincides to make the peaks of the incoming and outgoing meet, creating 'rogue' tide waves with exceptionally high tides. This is something that happens in the Bay of Fundy in Canada, home to the world's biggest tides.

Places with extreme tides tend to have a gradually sloping seabed. As you learnt on the last page, a small drop in the tide here exposes a vast area of intertidal zone; the same applies to a small rise in the tide that floods a large section of beach, travelling inland much faster than it would on a steeply sloping seabed. While the exposed tide uncovers a vast expanse to explore, you must be careful not to get caught out far from shore by a rapid rise in the tide; in some bays and estuaries this can come in the form of dangerous tidal bores (see Phenomena) charging over the sand and up rivers.

SMALL TIDES

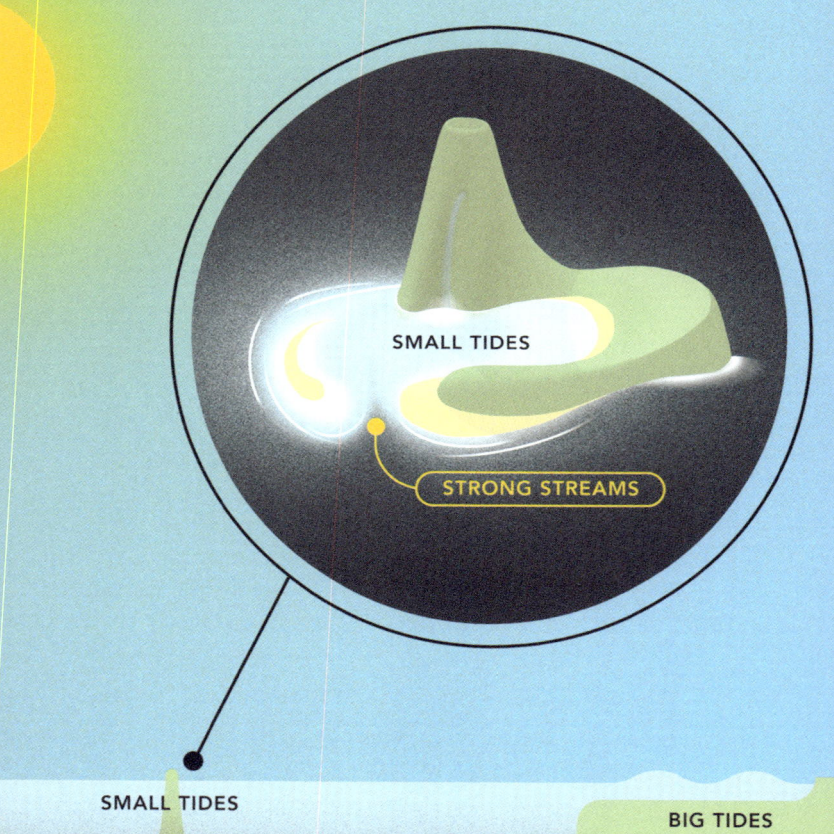

STRONG STREAMS

SMALL TIDES

BIG TIDES
CONTINENTAL SHELF

MID-OCEAN **ISLAND**

CONTINENTAL **SLOPE**

ABYSSAL **PLAIN**

Tides are usually bigger where the continental shelf is wider

The seabed of our oceans can be divided into two main parts; the abyssal plain (thousands of metres deep), and the continental shelf (hundreds of metres deep). As a general rule, the wider the continental shelf, the bigger the tides will be. This is based on the principle that waves travel faster in deeper water, so when tide waves reach the continental shelf they slow down and get compressed, growing in size and bringing higher tides. In contrast, places with a narrow continental shelf experience small tides because the tide wave travels past uninterrupted by water depth.

Common places with small tides are mid-ocean islands because they typically rise up steeply from the abyssal plain. Despite having a minimal vertical range from high to low water, you must still pay attention to the tides in these places because they often have lagoons with narrow entrances that experience a large volume of water pouring through every six hours. This creates strong tidal streams that can have a huge effect on when it is safe to enter or exit the lagoon (you can learn more about this in the *Tidal Streams Explorer Guide*).

SMALL TIDES

STRONG STREAMS

Some large seas have almost no tides

The secret is to look at where the sea meets the ocean and see how narrow the entrance is, because the main reason a sea will have minimal tides is if the entrance is too tight for the tide wave to push through. The Mediterranean is a perfect example of this; as the Atlantic tide wave races up from Africa to Europe, the 8-mile wide Straits of Gibraltar essentially blocks it from travelling freely in. So despite measuring 3,900km by 1,600km, the Med has a reputation for being 'tideless' with average ranges of just 30cm (although the channel between Europe and Africa has a unique mix of currents and tidal streams).

Despite places like the Mediterranean having an inconsequential vertical tide, there will be pockets where the tide must still be respected because a small tidal range can be amplified into powerful tidal streams, just like with lagoons in mid-ocean islands. The key geographical feature to look out for is a constriction between two large bodies of water; this could be a narrow channel between a 'loch' and the open sea, or a gap between the mainland and an island, such as the Straits of Messina connecting Italy to Sicily.

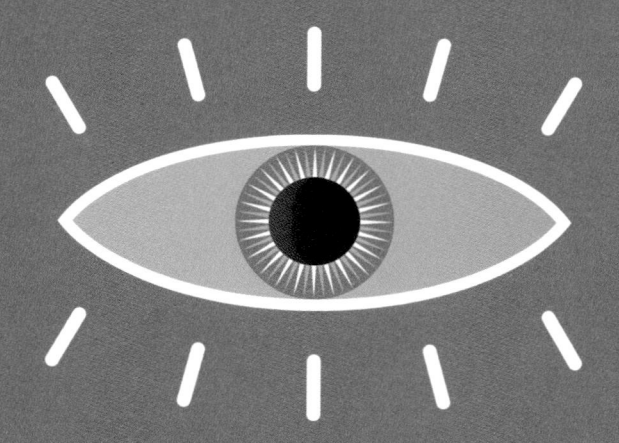

CLUES

FOR THE EXPLORER

The long periods between peaks and troughs of tide waves makes it difficult to see what the tide is doing at any moment in time. But if you look carefully, there are clues everywhere telling you whether it is high water or low, if the sea is rising or falling.

In this section we will explore the clues on beaches, in harbours and out at sea that are telling you what the tide is doing.

Take a note of the moon phase

By observing the moon phase you can predict the tide times and intensity. Here's how:

The moon in this illustration is a 'Waxing Crescent' (learn why in *The Moon Explorer Guide*), which happens when it is halfway between the New Moon and First Quarter. At this time of the lunar month the tides are strong because it has just been springs - but over the next week they will be getting weaker, with neaps 36 hours after the First Quarter. This means that with every coming day over the following week high tide will get a little lower, low tide will be slightly higher and streams will become less intense.

Because tides are the same at the New and Full Moon, if you remember the time of high tide at the Full Moon you can predict the tide times on any day of the lunar month by noting how many days before or after these phases it is and subtracting or adding 50 minutes per day from your memorised time. For example, if the high tide on your local beach is at midday on the New Moon, on the day of this illustration it will be around 2:30 (50 mins. x 3 days = approx. 2.5 hours).

TIDE TIP
FISHING BOATS ARE USUALLY KEPT ABOVE THE STORM HIGH TIDE

STORM SURGE HIGH TIDE

TODAY'S HIGH TIDE

OLD DETRITUS

Sand is **rough** above today's tide

Sand is **smooth** below recent high tide

WET SAND INDICATES TIDE IS FALLING

NEW DETRITUS

Look for lines of flotsam and jetsam

The highest line often indicates the last storm surge, when astronomical and meteorological factors conspired to create an exceptionally high tide. This line may be emphasised by a small cliff in the sand where waves cut away at the beach.

Beneath the storm surge line is the denser spring tide line, made by the last spring high within the past fortnight. If it is low tide and this is the only layer of flotsam and jetsam on the beach, you can be confident that it is currently springs. But if there are several lines of seaweed along the beach, it is likely to be neaps with each line marking a successive high tide slightly lower than the one the previous day.

If the beach is facing the sun and when you feel the seaweed it is still moist, the tide is probably falling (depending on the drying power of the sun). However, the longer the seaweed sits in the sun the more it dries out, and this indicates more time has passed since the last high tide. If the sea is near the high tide line, accurately observing whether it is rising or falling can make a huge difference to your prediction, with the next high tide either being in 1 hour or 11 hours time.

HIGH SPRING TIDE   **LOW** SPRING TIDE

Check the steepness of pontoons

Pontoons rise and fall with the tide, providing a valuable guide to what is happening. Here are the key features to look out for:

The slope of the ramp connecting the pontoon to dry land helps you quickly spot if it is high or low tide. If the ramp is horizontal, it will be a high spring tide. If it is very steep, it will be a low spring tide.

The tops of the posts that keep the pontoons in place are designed to stay out of the water at all times, so should mark a level above the Highest Astronomical Tide (HAT). To make the posts easy to spot the tops are often painted white so a quick glance around the pontoons shows you that level.

The average high spring tide line is usually clearly visible on the posts as the point up to where a band of marine growth is visible. The paint is also often faded up to this level and there are marks where the rubber from the connection with the pontoon slides up and down as the pontoon rises and falls with the tide.

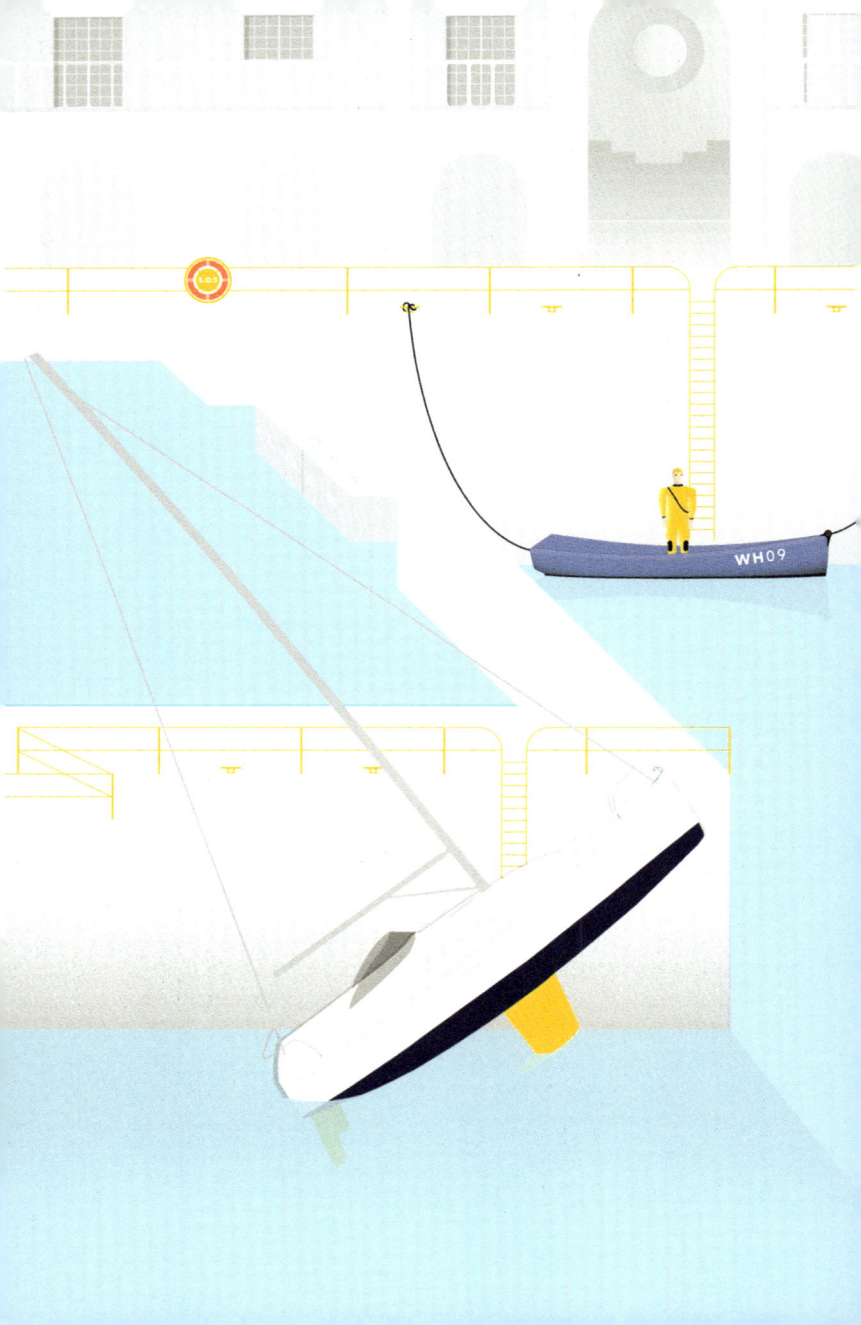

Observe the details around a harbour

If local boats have their mooring lines tight against the wall at high tide, with short bow and stern lines running perpendicular to the boat and quayside, you can be confident there is a minimal tidal range. But if all the ropes are running parallel to the harbour wall, with long bow and stern lines tied a long way from the front and back of the boat, expect a big drop at low tide.

A clear sign that a harbour dries out is an inner basin with a lock or sill to keep the water in. These are instantly obvious at low tide because of the different water levels on either side. But at high tide it is less apparent, so look carefully for signs of a lock gate or underwater sill in the narrowest part of the basin entrance.

At low tide, you can tell how high the sea gets by looking at wood bolted to the harbour wall. They are usually in good condition above the spring high tide, but start to show little holes below that point. Beneath the neap high tide line there is often signs of rotting, because it is submerged underwater at least twice every day. And like the pontoon posts the harbour wall will have a line of marine growth.

OPEN SEA > > >

Fishermen pitch their tents **above the high tide line**

Boats at anchor face into the stream, so the powerboat indicates the tide is falling because water is flowing out to sea

If you look closely on a calm day, you will see **water trickling up or down the beach**

Wet seaweed indicates the tide is falling

Watch the water

Looking at the water and spotting which way streams are flowing can help you predict the state of tide. If you look closely at the waterline you can sometimes actually see the tide rising or falling as it creeps up or down the shoreline – but this only works in extremely well protected areas where there is no swell. Creeks and natural harbours are the best place to see this happen and it works best on days with no wind because the only movement of water is the vertical rise or fall of the tide.

If there is flotsam and jetsam in the waterline, it is usually an indicator that the tide is rising because the detritus is being pushed up the beach. But if the waterline is free of any seaweed, driftwood (or sometimes sea foam) then the tide is likely falling, because everything has been deposited on the high water line.

Paying attention to which way the streams are flowing can help you work out if the tide is rising or falling. This works best in tidal rivers or estuaries because their cycle of streams means that water flows inland when the tide is rising and out to sea when the tide is falling.

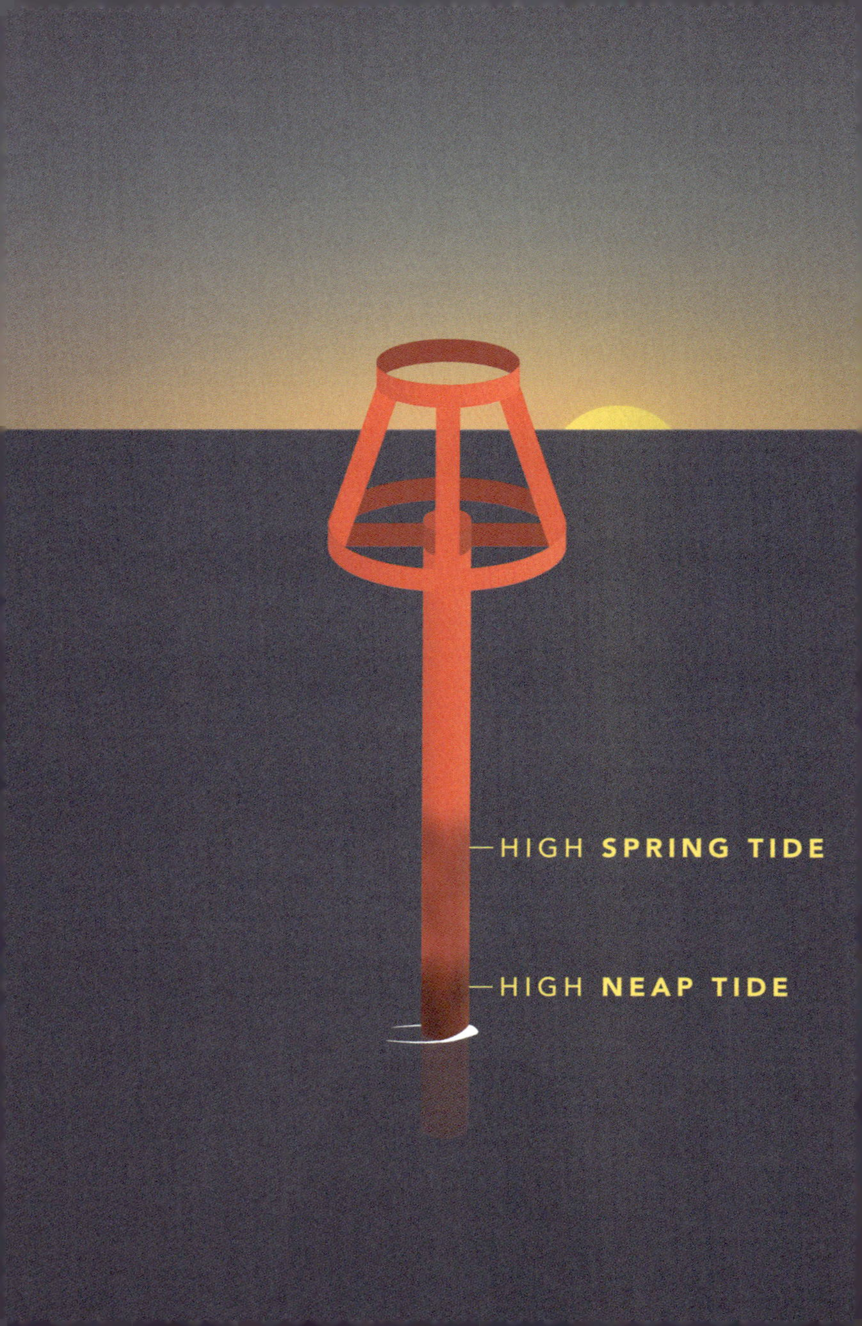
HIGH SPRING TIDE
HIGH NEAP TIDE

Pay attention to rocks, posts and cliffs

Engineered structures that protrude out to sea often have a post at their end, topped with what looks like an upside down basket. This is to let boats know that a submerged structure extends out to sea so they don't crash into it. For everyone else, it doubles up as a useful clue to see how far out the tide goes, because at low tide the base of the post is often out of the water. On a high spring tide this can seem like an unbelievably long way out, but remember that if the seabed slopes gently it takes just a small drop in the tide to expose a large area of beach.

When you see these posts at low tide (or any other metal structure) they provide a clear guide showing you how high the tide gets, indicated by the height the seaweed grows to. The thickest growth will be beneath the neap high tide line, and if you look closely you will see little barnacles growing up to the point where a high spring tide reaches.

On chalk cliffs there will be a dramatic line marking the high tide line, with bright white above the high spring tide and dark green with marine growth beneath that point.

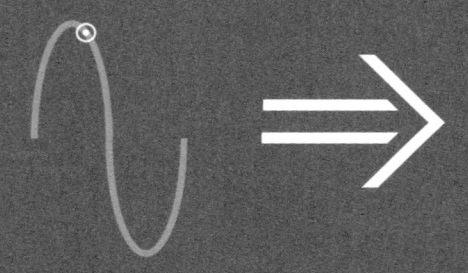

PHENOMENA
MADE BY TIDES

The tide creates two main phenomena, tidal bores and tidal streams. While bores are rare creatures that few people encounter, streams are common around most coastlines and have a huge impact on many of our adventures.

In this section we will explore how the tides makes these phenomena and discover where you can find them.

ESTUARY
FLOOD TIDE

BORE

WHEN BORE ARRIVES, BEACH RAPIDLY FLOODS

BORES CAN TRAVEL MANY MILES INLAND

Tides make Bores

Many rivers are tidal, with the tide rising up their banks for many miles inland. If this comes as a surprise, you'll be amazed to hear of 'bores', which are waves growing up to 10 metres high that rumble up a select number of tidal rivers around the world. The reason tidal bores are so rare is because they require specific conditions to evolve; the river should be wide, shallow, slow moving, and connected to a funnel-shaped estuary with big tides. The theory goes that as the tide rises in the estuary it is held back at a choke point until the pressure builds so great that the tide bursts forward as a single wave followed by a rapid rise in the water level.

The power of a bore is connected to the tidal range, so many will only form around springs when the range between high and low tide is greatest. Perigean spring tides will result in the biggest bores, especially if there is low air pressure and onshore winds. Rainfall also plays an important role because if there has been heavy rain upstream the river will have too strong a downward flow, reducing the upward movement of the bore. This is why some bores, like the Mascaret in southwest France, only form in the summer when the river has less rainwater flowing downstream.

At the *peak* (high tide) streams flow the **same way** as the tide wave

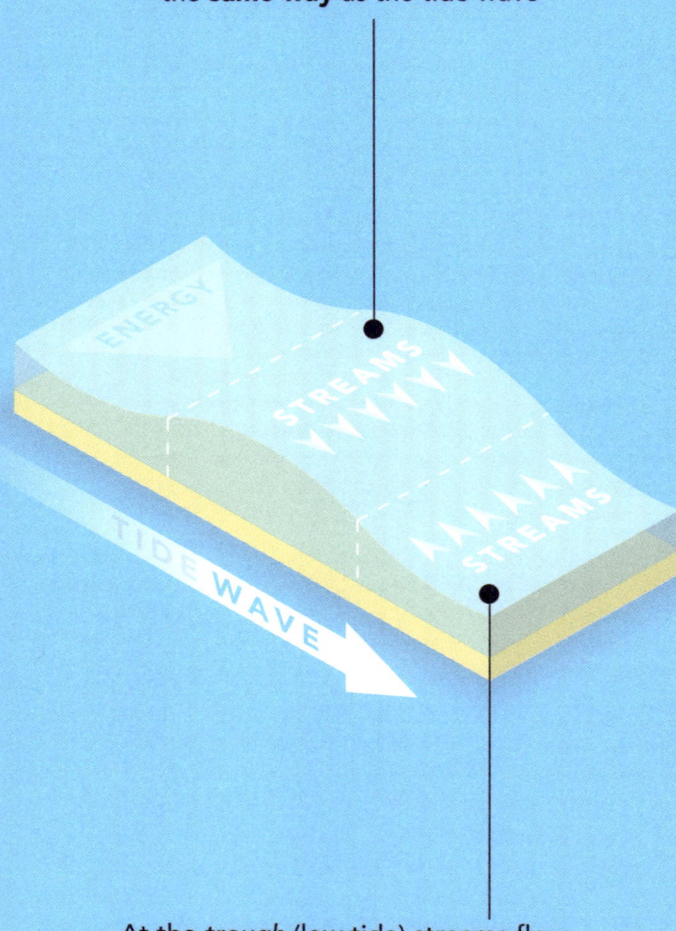

At the *trough* (low tide) streams flow the **opposite way** to the tide wave

Tides make Tidal Streams

Tide waves racing along the shore in shallow coastal waters make currents called tidal streams that flow both ways along the beach. The best way to understand the relationship between the energy in the wave and the currents is to imagine a tsunami. When a tsunami is approaching land, a clear sign is water draining from the beach; this is because the trough has arrived and although the energy in the wave is travelling towards you, currents are being sucked towards the peak, so travel in the opposite direction to the wave. But when the peak arrives, currents are pushed along with the wave and water surges up the beach.

Now take that concept and spin it 90 degrees so the wave is travelling along the shore. If it moves from left to right, at high tide on an open coast you would expect streams to be flowing to the right because they are being pushed along with the peak of the tide wave. But at low tide, they will be travelling the opposite direction to the wave, flowing to the left as they are being sucked towards the next incoming peak. This can be a big concept to digest, which is why we explain everything you need to know in the *Tidal Streams Explorer Guide*.

A
B
C

TIDE DICTIONARY

Amphidromic Point
A no-tide point from which co-tidal lines radiate

Apogean Neap Tide
A neap tide that happens when the moon is at apogee

Atmospheric Pressure
The weight of air, commonly called 'air pressure'. High pressure indicates cold air sinking (increasing the weight of air) and low pressure indicates warm air rising (decreasing the weight of air)

Bathymetry
The shape of the seabed

Bore
A rare river wave that happens mostly around spring tides in estuaries with big tides connected to shallow and slow moving rivers

Continental Shelf
Shallow waters close to continents

Co-tidal Line
A line extending from an Amphidromic Point where all places experience high tide at the same time

Diurnal Tide
A tidal cycle with just one high tide a day, notably the Gulf of Mexico and Western Australia

Double High Tide
When two high tides happen in close succession, usually 1-3 hours apart

Ebb Tide
The part of the tidal cycle from high tide to low tide, when the tide is falling

Equinox
A twice-yearly event when north and south poles are equal distances from the sun

Flood Tide
The part of the tidal cycle from low tide to high tide, when the tide is rising

HAT / LAT
'Highest/Lowest Astronomical Tide'; the highest/lowest tide a place experiences when all astronomical factors coincide, such as a perigean spring tide at the equinox when the moon has a low declination.

High Water
The formal way to describe a day's high tide

Jetsam
Objects jettisoned overboard deliberately, as opposed to Flotsam which is accidental debris

King Tide
A colloquial name for a perigean spring tide

Low Water
The formal way to describe a day's low tide

MHWS / MLWS
Mean High/Low Water Springs; the average height of high/low water at spring tides

MHWN / MLWN
Mean High/Low Water Neaps; the average height of high/low water at neap tides

Mixed Tides
A type of semi-diurnal cycle where one high tide (or low tide) is higher than the other

Neaps
Weak tides that happen 36 hours after the First Quarter and Third Quarter moon phases

Perigean Spring Tide
A powerful spring tide that happens when the moon is at perigee

Range Of Tide
The height difference between high and low tide

Resonance
A bathtub-like phenomena in a bay or estuary where the outgoing high tide merges with the incoming high tide to form an extra high tide

Semi-Diurnal Tide
A tidal cycle with two high tides a day

Springs
Strong fortnightly tides that happen 36 hours after New Moon and Full Moon

Stand Of Tide
A condition at low or high tide when there is no vertical change in the tide

Storm Surge
When a high astronomical tide coincides with low atmospheric pressure and onshore winds to create extra high tides that put a coastline at risk of flooding

Tidal Streams
Currents flowing back and forth along a shore, generally changing direction every 6 hours at a set time before and after high tide

Tide Wave
A wave that travels around an ocean or sea (anti-clockwise in the northern hemisphere) bringing high water at the peaks and low water at the troughs

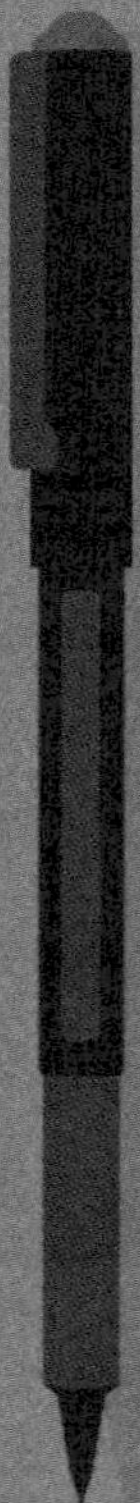

ADVENTURE PLANNER

If you run out of pages or don't want to write in this book, you can download the adventure planner template and print them yourself at **www.tidalcompass.com**

Date ....

Location ....

High Tide __:__ (__._m) & __:__ (__._m)

Low Tide __:__ (__._m) & __:__ (__._m)

Slack Water __:__ & __:__ & __:__

Streams flow ____ from __:__ to __:__

Streams flow ____ from __:__ to __:__

WIND

__:__   __:__   __:__   __:__   __:__

(N)   (N)   (N)   (N)   (N)

_ _   _ _   _ _   _ _   _ _
(_ _) (_ _) (_ _) (_ _) (_ _)

NOTES

Date ....

Location ....

High Tide __:__ (__.__m) & __:__ (__.__m)

Low Tide __:__ (__.__m) & __:__ (__.__m)

Slack Water __:__ & __:__ & __:__

Streams flow ____ from __:__ to __:__

Streams flow ____ from __:__ to __:__

WIND

__:__   __:__   __:__   __:__   __:__

(N)   (N)   (N)   (N)   (N)

 --   --   --   --   --
(__) (__) (__) (__) (__)

NOTES

Date ....

Location ....

High Tide __:__ (__.__m) & __:__ (__.__m)

Low Tide __:__ (__.__m) & __:__ (__.__m)

Slack Water __:__ & __:__ & __:__

Streams flow ____ from __:__ to __:__

Streams flow ____ from __:__ to __:__

WIND

__:__ __:__ __:__ __:__ __:__

(N) (N) (N) (N) (N)

\- \- \- \- \- \- \- \- \- \-
(__) (__) (__) (__) (__)

NOTES

More books in the series...

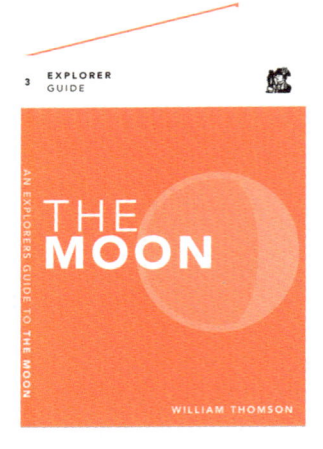

www.imray.com